Masterpieces: Artists and Their Works

Picasso

by Shelley Swanson Sateren

W

FRANKLIN WATTS

LONDON•SYDNEY

This edition first published in 2006 by

Franklin Watts
338 Euston Road
London
NW1 3BH

Franklin Watts Australia
Hachette Children's Books
Level 17/207 Kent Street
Sydney NSW 2000

ISBN-10: 0 7496 6932 2

ISBN-13: 978 0 7496 6932 4

© Capstone Press. 2002, 2004, 2006
Series created by Bridgestone Books, published by Capstone Press
151 Good Counsel Drive, P.O. Box 669, Mankato, Minnesota 56002

A CIP catalogue reference for this book is available from the British Library.

Printed in China

Consultant: Joan Lingen, Ph.D.Professor of Art History, Clarke College, Iowa, USA

Cover Art: *Woman with Raised Arms* by Pablo Picasso

Editorial Credits:
Blake Hoena, editor; Karen Risch, product planning editor; Heather Kindseth, cover
designer and interior designer; Katy Kudela, photo researcher

Photo Credits:
Art Resource, cover (left); Art Resource/Giraudon, 18; Fogg Art Museum, Harvard
University Art Museums, USA/Bequest from the Collection of Maurice Wertheim, Class
1906/Bridgeman Art Library, 8; Hulton/Archive/Getty Images, cover (right);
Mary and Leigh B. Block Charitable Foundation; restricted gift of Maymar Corporation and
Mrs. Maurice L Rothschild; through prior gift of Mr. and Mrs. Edwin E. Hokin;
Hertle fund, 1954.270. The Art Institute of Chicago, 20; Musee Picasso, Paris,
France/Bridgeman Art Library, 14; Museo Nacional Centro de Arte Reina Sofia, Madrid,
Spain/Bridgeman Art Library, 16; Museo Picasso, Barcelona, Spain/Bridgeman Art Library,
6; Private Collection/Roger-Viollet, Paris/Bridgeman Art Library, 4; Pushkin Museum,
Moscow, Russia/Bridgeman Art Library, 10; The Museum of Modern Art, New York.
Acquired through the Lillie P. Bliss Bequest, 12.

Table of Contents

Pablo worked on art almost every day of his life. He began
drawing at the age of two and painted until his death in 1973.

Pablo Picasso

Pablo Picasso (1881–1973) is one of the most important artists of the 20th century. He helped develop several new styles of art.

In about 1907, Pablo began an art movement called **Cubism**. Cubists flattened and simplified the shapes of the objects they painted. They often painted objects in sections. The different sections showed all sides of the objects.

Pablo helped invent new art methods such as **collage** and **assemblage**. He created a collage by attaching objects like newspaper and chicken wire to paintings. Assemblage is a type of **sculpture** which uses everyday objects. Pablo once used a bicycle seat and handlebars to make a bull's head and horns.

Pablo's experiments with art styles led to **abstract art**. In abstract art, people and objects do not often look life like. Artists just give an impression of them.

Pablo painted *First Communion* when he was 14 years old. The
man on the left side of the painting resembles Pablo's father, José.

Young Pablo

Pablo Ruiz y Picasso was born in Malaga, Spain, on 25th October 1881. His father's name was José Ruiz Blasco and his mother's name was María Picasso y Lopez.

José was an art teacher and a painter. He encouraged Pablo to draw and paint. He also signed Pablo up for art classes. At the age of 13, Pablo finished a painting of a pigeon that his father had started. After seeing the painting, José decided that Pablo was more talented than he was. He then decided to give up painting and concentrate on Pablo's art education.

José wanted Pablo to have a **classical art** education. Classical art is created in the style of ancient Greek and Roman art. It tries to show people and objects exactly the way they look.

However, Pablo wanted to work with different styles of art. In 1900, he decided to visit Paris, France, with his friend Carlos Casagemas. In Paris, artists were experimenting with new art styles.

This version of *Mother and Child* was painted during Pablo's Blue Period. The mother's hands and feet appear to be unnaturally long.

Blue Period

Casagemas died soon after the visit to Paris and Pablo moved to Barcelona, Spain. This was a hard time for Pablo. He was saddened by Casagemas's death and he was not selling many paintings. He often had no money for food or art supplies. He even had to burn some of his drawings to keep warm.

This time of Pablo's life became known as his Blue Period (1901–1904). During his Blue Period, Pablo used a great deal of blue in his paintings. Blue is considered to be the colour of sadness.

The colour blue seemed to suit the people Pablo painted. He painted people suffering from loneliness and hunger. He often painted beggars and poor people.

Pablo began to develop his own style during his Blue Period. He did not make people look real in his paintings. Instead, he would paint them with extra long fingers, arms and legs. He made their bodies thin and bony and their faces often looked like masks.

Pablo painted this version of *The Family of Saltimbanques* (comedians) in 1905. The figure on the left side of the painting may be a **self portrait**.

Rose Period

In 1904, Pablo decided to move to Paris. He met many artists and writers there. He often went to cafés and parties to talk about art and writing with them.

During this time, Pablo met and fell in love with Fernande Olivier. His mood soon improved and he no longer felt as sad. His paintings also changed to reflect this new happiness. He began to paint with reds, pinks and oranges instead of blues. This change marked the beginning of his Rose Period (1904–1905).

The subjects Pablo painted also changed. Many of his paintings during this time showed jesters, circus acrobats and clowns.

Art collectors were more interested in Pablo's Rose Period paintings than his Blue Period paintings. They preferred the happier subjects and colours. Pablo began to sell more paintings and was soon earning enough money to live comfortably.

Pablo was studying African masks when he painted *Les Demoiselles d'Avignon*. The two women on the right have faces that look like African masks.

Cubism

In 1907, Pablo painted *Les Demoiselles d'Avignon*. Many people did not understand this painting. They thought it was strange. Pablo had painted the women's bodies in flat shapes.

George Braque was one of the few people who praised Pablo's painting. At the time, Braque and Pablo were experimenting with similar ways of painting. Soon, they were painting together and sharing ideas.

Braque and Pablo began the Cubist art movement. In their paintings, Cubists broke people, objects and landscapes up into simple shapes. These shapes often looked like building blocks. The artists then put the shapes together in different ways, so that they might show the front, back and sides of an object or person all at one time.

Pablo often painted two eyes on one side of a person's face and moved the mouth and nose around. This allowed him to show the front and sides of a person's face at the same time.

Pablo used a rope to frame *Still Life with Caned Chair*. The bottom left section of this collage is a piece of cloth that looks like part of a chair.

Collage

In 1917, Pablo met the Russian ballerina Olga Koklova while working on the ballet *Parade*. *Parade* was about circus people. Pablo had agreed to make the sets and costumes for the ballet.

Pablo's relationship with Fernande had ended in 1911. In 1918, Olga and Pablo got married. They had a son 3 years later, whom they named Paulo.

In the 1920s, most art **critics** and dealers had accepted Cubism. People bought many of Pablo's paintings. He was becoming one of the most successful artists of the time.

Pablo continued to experiment with art styles. One day, he would paint a Cubist painting. The next day, he might create a painting in a classical style.

Pablo's experimentation led him to collage. Collage comes from the French word *coller* which means to paste. Pablo began to glue real objects, such as newspaper, rope or cloth, to his paintings. The images he painted in his collages were not life like, but he tried to make them look real by pasting these real objects to them.

Guernica is 3.5 metres by 7.8 metres tall. The painting shows a
dying horse and a woman in a burning building. On the left side
of the painting, a mother screams as she holds her dead child.

Guernica

Pablo and Olga had a troubled marriage. They often argued and Pablo eventually left her.

In 1927, Pablo met Marie-Thérèse Walter. In 1935, they had a daughter named Maya.

In 1936, civil war broke out in Spain. Several Spanish military leaders attacked the Spanish government. German leaders helped the Spanish military leaders. In 1937, German pilots bombed Guernica, Spain. About 2,000 people died during this attack.

Pablo supported the Spanish government. He sent money to Spain to help people suffering because of the war. Pablo was angry about the bombing and his feelings of anger inspired him to paint *Guernica*.

In *Guernica*, Pablo showed the horrors of war. He used only black, white and grey paint, as he felt these colours represented death and destruction. In 1937, *Guernica* was displayed at the World's Fair in Paris. It is one of Pablo's most famous paintings.

Pablo used a ball to make the ape's body for the statue *The Ape and Her Young.* He used coffee cup handles for the ears.

Assemblage

In 1943, Pablo met Françoise Gilot. She and Pablo had two children together. Claude was born in 1947 and Paloma was born in 1949. However, Françoise left Pablo in 1953.

In 1954, Pablo met Jacqueline Roque. In 1961, they married. Pablo spent the rest of his life with her.

During the 1950s and 1960s, Picasso created a new type of sculpture called assemblage. Sculptors usually carved statues from rock or formed them from clay, but Picasso used everyday objects to create his sculptures. He used forks, bicycle seats, pieces of wood or other objects that he found. Assemblage is also known as *objets trouvés*, or found-object art.

His son's toy car inspired him to make the sculpture *The Ape and Her Young*. The car was the ape's head and marbles in the car's front windows were the eyes. Pablo showed that everyday objects could be turned into art.

In 1921, Pablo painted this version of *Mother and Child*. He created this painting in a classical art style. He also made the figures appear as if they were made out of stone.

Picasso's Fame

Due to his fame, Pablo was often asked to paint special works of art. In the 1950s, officials from the United Nations asked him to paint a wall in its new building in Paris. The United Nations is an organisation that works to prevent war around the world. The wall was 10 metres square. Pablo made the painting on 40 separate panels and then had the panels placed on the wall.

In 1967, Pablo's painting *Mother and Child* sold for $500,000 (roughly £315,000). No other living artist had ever received this much money for one work of art.

Pablo died at his home in Mougins, France on 8th April 1973. He was 91 years old. Pablo worked on a painting the night before he died.

Today, many museums own Pablo's paintings and sculptures. Both Paris and Barcelona have art museums dedicated to him.

Timeline

1881 – Pablo is born in Spain on 25th October.

1901 – Pablo's Blue Period begins.

1904 – Pablo's Rose Period begins.

1907 – Pablo paints *Les Demoiselles d'Avignon*; this painting is considered the first Cubist painting.

1914 – World War I begins.

1918 – Pablo marries Olga Koklova.

1921 – Pablo's son Paulo is born.

1935 – Pablo's daughter Maya is born.

1937 – Town of Guernica is bombed; Pablo paints *Guernica*.

1939 – World War II begins.

1947 – Pablo's son Claude is born.

1949 – Pablo's daughter Paloma is born.

1961 – Pablo marries Jacqueline Roque.

1973 – Pablo dies on 8th April.

Useful Websites

www.home.xnet.com/~stanko/
This award-winning Picasso website is a great interactive site, full of information and easy-to-see paintings and sculptures.

www.tamu.edu/mocl/picasso/
An innovative website which gives lots of information on Picasso, as well as instructions and advice on how to create your own Picasso-style art.

www.whytownps.sa.edu.au/visarts/
This Australian school website looks at many different artists, including Cubists, and explores their various styles of art. Provides a range of art activities and quizzes.

www.tate.org.uk/
The Tate Modern's website takes users on a virtual tour of their fantastic galleries. It includes a range of Picasso's art, as well as work from many other excellent artists.

www.moma.org/
The Museum of Modern Art in New York provides this website for users to view their galleries online. It includes a good collection of Picasso's works.

Note to parents and teachers
Every effort has been made by the Publishers to ensure that these websites are suitable for children; that they are of the highest educational value, and that they contain no inappropriate or offensive material. However, because of the nature of the Internet, it is impossible to guarantee that the contents of these sites will not be altered. We strongly advise that Internet access is supervised by a responsible adult.

Glossary

abstract art – a style of art which does not attempt to be life like

assemblage – an art form using everyday objects to make sculptures

classical art – in the style of ancient Greek or Roman art

collage – a picture made by gluing pieces of materials, such as paper or cloth, to a surface

critic – someone who reviews art, books or films

Cubism – an art style in which artists break objects, people and landscapes into simple shapes

sculpture – a three-dimensional work of art

self portrait – a piece of artwork which an artist creates of himself or herself

Index